My Journal

_____

CHANGE

POETRY JOURNAL

Poetry by KAS Sartori
Design by William Withrow

KBW CREATIVE PUBLISHING
LOS ANGELES

Other Books by
Kas Sartori

The Chosen Shell
LOVE, Poetry Journal

CHANGE, Poetry Journal
is a book of poetry by Kas Sartori with journal pages
Design by William Withrow
Published by KBW Creative Publishing
First Edition October 2024
Copyright 2024 by Kas Sartori, www.kassartori.com

ISBN 979-8-9918187-1-1

Dedication

For all those, whatever age,
who challenge themselves to grow and
change. Whether taking risks and "going for it" or
grappling with an unexpected life challenge,
these are people who ignore their fears and
turn their vision and diligence into triumph.

Poetry

expresses our deepest, most profound emotions.

Stringing words together and laying them down in this
journal daily, weekly, monthly can illuminate our
feelings, our struggles, our ever-changing life path. Plus,
playing with words can be magical! By free-writing our
thoughts, we'll come to know ourselves better, the
journey of change in our own lives, the trembling fear
that attacks us, and the steps we're willing to risk to go
forward and capture our dreams.

Change

a word that's filled with infinite meanings.

Read my poems, then choose words on the next page and recall the shifts and turns in your own life. Remember the struggles and exuberance of reinventing yourself. Record the tumultuous emotions a change foisted on you. Did you wish you'd never taken a path less traveled? Did you plunge into changes, naive and unprepared? Did you accept an unexpected turn in the road and transform it into joy? Play with your words and create precious memories of those unforgettable moments.

Soar

Walk Away

Expand ⚜ Act

Regenerate ⚜ Birth

Rekindle ⚜ Transform

Turn Over A New Leaf

Substitute ⚜ Restore

Disintegrate ⚜

Cancel ⚜ Disappear ⚜

Adapt ⚜ Reduce

Sprout ⚜ Leap

Free To Fly

Start

Bounce Back

Revive ⚜ Grow

Move On ⚜ Remove

Take off & Landing

Subtract ⚜ Increase

Diversify ⚜ Gain

Shift ⚜ Alter

Turn the Tide

Rebirth ⚜ Mature

Enlarge ⚜ Restore

Develop

Dancing Wings

Oh, Butterfly, I watch you swerve and flutter and flit
midst bushes, trees and flowers galore,
envisioning your journey from
a creeping creature with numerous legs
to a chrysalis,
a silent case hanging still for weeks.
    And then a wild and wonderful transformation!
    Did you ever imagine you'd change so much?
Exploding with
    silken, effervescent wings and a life of fluttering,
    reminding me of
        a windy dance of joy!

Oh, Butterfly, with wings so soft,
now every day you fly aloft
and wisk away wherever you may...
    Isn't This...
        the pinnacle of living?

                                KAS

14

The Dreaming Fields

Come relax with me in butterfly fields, envisioning
who else you might be...where you might go.
Listen to your whispered wishes.
They will lead you there. Do you want to write? lead?
paint? dance? create? make a difference?
   I've wandered through the years myself, searching
for my inner voice, journeying through darkness
and light, closing life's doors and opening others.

Through myriad dawns and sunsets,
I've reinvented myself and my dreams.
Because life is all about growing, isn't it?
...and its circuitous paths that lead us to
               our own personal contentment
                  ...for a while at least,
until we feel compelled to reinvent ourselves
again...
      and yet again.

                              KAS

Imagination

Imagination

Imagination

Imagination

Reborn

Sitting by the sea.
Amber kelp heaps lying near,
with seagulls close enough
  to me
I feel
  my own sensations
    finally,
like seagulls inside new eggs
cracking open
  with fledgling wings
  wet within
  hoping soon
  to flutter and fly...
And now
a seagull
    slides by
shifting motion in the wind
so close
I feel its breeze!

Oh, to fly to your frontiers,
ride your tail past
  doubts I've thrown away,
  old hopes cast aside
  and a sorrowing heart
  ...soon be stitched.

Oh, to fly with you...
and find horizons hidden within,
  quenching a new thirst!

                    KAS

Regeneration

the sun sets...the sun rises

but not before night intrevenes

permitting

the slow painful pause

necessary

to end

    and begin again

                KAS

Free-Write

Free-Write

Free-Write

Free-Write

Greenland's Lesson

Oldest island in the world
    what can you teach me?
Is your ancient movement up the globe
    through centuries of time a lesson...
    that I must not count on fixed stars
                or familiar loves?

For as a land mass travels
    and transforms over time,
so do we.
And as certain as a sunrise
    promises a new day,
    the breath and the beat of our lives
    will shift into new rhythms,
    even
        traversing to a world
           beyond ours.

                    KAS

Walk Away

I can't care anymore.
I can't care anymore so much
    that when it's time to fly, though
my heart whispers about sky and clouds
    and lacy waves leaning toward shore,
        I shift back toward you.

I can't care anymore so much
    that I try to find the
        smile you've lost and buried.

I can't care so much that I stay with the man I loved,
    postponing, refraining, waiting...until the sun sets
        and night keeps me captured
            as you brood.
No, I can't care that much anymore!
                        I must fly or die.

                                    KAS

Journal

Journal

Journal

Journal

Release

Switch and shift,
Swing into new phases,
　　　old dreams.
Close doors.
Reconnect.
Open wide the tried and true places
　　　that bring joy.

Get out of the groove,
Stop the forced flow of words.
Incessant stream
　　of projects, deadlines,
　　　achievements forged by shoulds.
Need to fly, Need to swing, Need to rush out,
　　play with the wind,
　　　stare at the sky...
　　　　feel the flow
　　　　　begin again...

KAS

37

Autumn's Transformation

Enjoy these bursts of red and yellow, green and brown.
They celebrate a year of life and grief and joy.
Multicolored memories of
       milestones
        where we grew close
                and closer still.
But now, as weathered leaves detach
so do we, from certainty and expectation,
moving into crisper, colder breezes
and early darkness
where our path leads out to who knows where.
Still,
celebrate we must,
lifting leaves from piles we've made,
we watch them fly and soar away
     in the gentle rise of Autumn's breath and
       light upon the fertile earth where they disappear
       eventually, to be born again.
       Like us.   **KAS**

Word-Play

Word-Play

Word-Play

Word-Play

New Beginning

Break the chains of yearning
Sever those desires
Block your mind's churning
Admit you're left out

How many times
    will they uninvite you
Before you cease this rage?
Silence your secret longings
Unlock your cage.

My mind knows my failings:
Belong no matter what
Desire borne of childhood
Pining for what is not.

Thoughts recreates us
Vision makes us free,
A robin flying solo
Is buoyed up by the breeze.

Erase your mind's wondering:
Why do they leave me out?
Find friends who nurture.
Go seek them out.

A tiny wren should venture
out of the family nest,
Trying to find adventure,
putting itself to a test...
rather than stay enfolded
in a stifling nest.

Fly
  With others
    Soar high!

                  KAS

Hidden Future

I gaze out at hills, far distant...
knowing not which path I'll take
    a darkened hole within...a hole where worry aches.
And I can't help but wonder: Is tragedy ahead,
    filled with tearful, trudging steps? Going where?
Or can I banish useless thoughts that poison me within
    and gaze instead at glorious dawn
that lights those far-off hills,
while still believing
    the open swing of breezes,
    that tempt me forward, despite a toxic path,
    will offer promises of future joy?
But no, there *are* no guarantees
    of either tears or smiles
I simply have this moment, this present,
this amazing day to offer love and
    prayers for mine and others' needs.

KAS

Poetry

Poetry

Poetry

Poetry

DISCOVER

THE MAGIC OF WRITING

Whether you love to write or not, I predict this journal will entice you to imagine your own memories and feelings about changes in your life. Then, with your laptop or pen, you'll kickstart your own unique muse.

Select a poem from this book. Read it and reread it, then...

🌼 **Free-write:** On a blank page, jot down a few Change-words from page 11. Add your own phrases. Fill the page with your random musings.

🌼 **Imagine & Word-Play:** Picture a memory. Choose a phrase or two to paint that scene. Pick more words to express your feelings.

🌼 **Journal & Poetry:** Stop and breathe. Read your creation. Add more phrases. Read it aloud. It doesn't have to be perfect! This is your own precious poem.

When your paragraph or poem is finished, add it to the CHANGE journal. You'll be surprised at the secrets your writing will reveal to you!

The Road Not Taken

"...I shall be telling this with a sigh
Somewhere ages and ages hence:
Two roads diverged in a wood, and I-
I took the one less traveled by,
And that has made all the difference."

Robert Frost

Made in the USA
Las Vegas, NV
22 April 2025